DESIGNING WITH vellum

by Robin Johnson

Text by Dan Maryon

OVER 150 IDEAS FOR SCRAPBOOKS, CARD MAKING, GIFTS AND MORE.

The Sophisticated Scrapbook

An Imprint of Autumn Leaves

Acknowledgements

"Designing With Vellum" is the first in a series of books
published under the imprint, "The Sophisticated Scrapbook,"
a division of Autumn Leaves.

The Sophisticated Scrapbook,
A Division of Autumn Leaves,
Encino, California
Design Director: Jeff Lam
Designers On This Book Include
Emilio Medina and Leaf Bainbridge

Front Cover Artwork: Robin Johnson
Text By Dan Maryon

For information about bulk sales or promotional pricing,
contact Josie Cartellone at Autumn Leaves: 1-800-588-6707

Words cannot adequately express the gratitude I feel for all those who have helped this book become a reality!

My deepest thanks to my loving and patient husband, Andrew. I have adored him since I was 13! He has been there for me day and night and I am so grateful that he has always encouraged my goals and dreams. He is an incredible man and I appreciate all he has sacrificed for this book.

My four wonderful children have been my biggest fans and I love them. Clairissa, Lizzie, Sarah, and Devin – you are the reason I love scrapbooking! I could never have too many memories of your precious lives.

Many thanks to Jeff Lam, Josie and the staff of Autumn Leaves. They have been a pleasure to work with and always encouraging. I appreciate their design skills that gave this book life. I am also grateful for our copywriter, Dan Maryon, whose talents and skill brought expression to all that you will see.

I am so grateful for my parents and siblings: Mom, Dad, Annie, Ed, Beth, Dan, Don, Kris and Janie. They have been my strength and my friends. I have been so blessed in my life to be surrounded by their loving examples. They are humble, wonderful people who have taught me to search for all that is good in life.

For all my friends who have enriched my life in so many ways – thank you! I am especially indebted to Rhonda Solomon for her creative ideas and laughter; to Julie Reeves for her inspiration and talents, and to Martha Johansen for all the memories and double stuffed Oreos.

I could not have completed this book without the contributions of so many talented artists: Debbie Crouse was a lifesaver with her ideas and vision for the last chapters of the book. The talents of Sharon Lewis, Rhonda Solomon, Candice Cook, Laurie Quinn, and Michelle Yaksick have also added much to the book. I am fortunate to call you my friends! I also appreciate all those who loaned their precious photographs to me.

Finally, to those who have helped me professionally: Paula Kraeme, Shauna Bomar, Kyle Poulin, and Don, Phil and the PrinTeam crew. Thank you for your unwavering support and belief in me.

Robin Johnson

Welcome!

I remember the first time I saw vellum in my local scrapbook store. I was amazed. I was enthralled! The sheer qualities were so enchanting and so different than the cardstock and printed paper I had always used. It was definitely love at first sight — I couldn't wait to go home and create something with it.

Since that time, I have used vellum in literally hundreds of layouts and projects. I also developed three product lines that are created with vellum. It continues to amaze and inspire me! It is so beautiful and versatile. At times it seems chameleon-like, changing to meet the look of every project I do.

When I used vellum for the first time, there were two kinds to choose from: light weight and heavy weight clear vellum. Today there are endless possibilities on the market: there is an entire rainbow of solid color vellum to work with and more patterned, metallic, and embossed vellum than I ever could have imagined.

The possibilities are only limited by your imagination, so don't hold back. Be creative! Try something new. My hope is that this book becomes a springboard for you to create amazing things. Have fun, and discover for yourself the reason I think working with vellum can be... sheer bliss.

contents

Adhesives

Adhering vellum is often the biggest problem people experience while working with it. Vellum's strength is also its weakness: the same sheer quality that lets you see through to the background also lets you see the big blotches of glue. So what can you do? There are several options.

Whenever someone asks me, "what is the best adhesive for vellum?" I always answer that my favorite adhesive is no adhesive at all. There are so many other great things on the market that will work to secure vellum. Try these for starters:

- Tying it with ribbon
- Dangling it with eyelets
- Hand stitching it or using a sewing machine
- Hanging it with wire
- Holding it in place with a button
- Using brads or fasteners
- Using paper ties

Look at the sample squares at the bottom of this page. Not one of them uses any adhesive.

Another solution that often works for me is to plan my project first. This applies mostly to scrapbooking. Say, for instance, that I wanted to use a patterned vellum for my background paper. I would design and prepare my page without adhering anything. Then once I am done planning, I start on the top layer and work down. I adhere the photos, title, die-cuts, etc., to the vellum. Then I flip the bottom layer of vellum over. Wherever it is covered by any of those pieces, I put photo tabs underneath. I can then flip it back over and secure the vellum to the cardstock background.

For both of these solutions, the edges of the vellum will still be loose. That may or may not be a problem for you. Each project or page will have different adhesive needs, and each solution has pros and cons. Judge your project based on the needs of the piece. Here are some good questions to ask:

Can the vellum be loose on the edges? Generally, if a scrapbook page is in a sheet protector, it isn't a problem. If you're doing a craft that will hang on the wall, you'll probably want it secured.

Does this need to be a strong permanent hold or should it be repositionable? Sometimes I am unsure of the placement of things. I want to be able to move my vellum around or remove it if it doesn't work out. Other times, I know exactly what I'm doing and want a permanent, secure solution.

Is this a temporary solution? Some projects just aren't long term, so I may not go to the extra effort that some adhesives require. Or my adhesive may only need to hold something in place until I can secure it later.

If you decide that your project needs to have an adhesive, here are some tips, techniques, and suggestions to help ensure your success. These comments are based on my personal experience with the products and do not represent Autumn Leaves or the product manufacturers.

Xyron Machine

If you use a lot of vellum, a Xyron is a must. The size you use (12" width, 8.5" width, or a smaller sticker/label maker) depends on your needs. I have an 8.5" wide machine and use it for things that need a permanent hold. This book's cover design is a good example: I wanted the layers to be very secure and I knew just what I wanted it to look like. Xyron is also excellent for die-cut pieces or punches. You can put all those little things through the machine and it works like a charm — they come out like stickers. Xyron has two types of adhesive to fit your needs: repositionable or permanent.

Two extra Tips: when you lay a light piece of Xyron-backed vellum over a dark background, it can look a little mottled. Test a scrap of vellum first to see if there is a color change. Also, there are times when the adhesive may build up around the edges. This extra adhesive can easily be removed by using a rubber cement pick-up square from a local art supply store. Otherwise, I give a Xyron a "two thumbs up" — as you'll see in the product lists, it was used on many pieces.

Double Sided Tape

Tape is perfect for many non-scrapbooking needs. I use it for bags, envelopes, and craft projects. It works well for projects that need a strong hold on the seam. It is slightly visible, but for those type of projects this usually doesn't bother me.

Spray Adhesive

This is another great choice for your projects. A spray adhesive provides a nice coat of glue without showing through. The other thing I love is that it is repositionable. I usually tend to change my mind as I work, so this is a great solution. There are a few things you should know if you use a spray adhesive. It is an aerosol, like spray paint, so you need to always spray it outside, not in your house or in a store. Go outside and place your vellum on some scratch paper. Hold the can upside down and spray away from your vellum to clear the nozzle (sometimes it will clog and then splatter when you try to spray it). Hold the can about 18 inches away for the best coating. If you spray too close and cover the vellum with too much glue, set it aside for a while and it will become less tacky. After you're done, turn the can upside down again and spray to clear the nozzle.

Adhesive Mounting Sheets

To use the adhesive sheets, first press the vellum onto the sheet and then cut it out. Next, peel back the bottom layer of the mounting sheet. Now your vellum is coated with adhesive. The only drawback is that you have to cut the object out after it is put on the adhesive sheet. If you have an intricate piece this can be time consuming.

Clear Mounting Tabs

Clear mounting tabs are similar to double-sided tape but are already cut into tabs. I would not use them on a plain colored vellum, but if your vellum has a pattern to it, it may not show through. I like using it for other projects like cards and tags.

Glue Stick

A glue stick is helpful for certain situations. Although a glue stick can sometimes show through vellum, it is better than any liquid glue I have found on the market. Use a thin application of it and use it for things that are less permanent — cards, tags, envelopes, etc. Sometimes I'll use a glue stick while scrapbooking to hold something down until I can use a more permanent adhesive later.

For my personal set-up at home, I have one of each of these products that I have mentioned. I have never had a vellum project that I couldn't find the right adhesive for. In this book, where possible, we have listed the adhesive used on each project. If no adhesive is listed, check to see if it was secured with something else (a ribbon, brads, etc.). When we list photo tabs as the adhesive, it means I planned my page first, and then used tabs under my page pieces.

Now that you know all the solutions to adhesives, I hope you feel completely free to create!

Design Tips

As I've taught scrapbooking workshops and classes, I've used my background in graphic design to answer many questions about page design. Because there's nothing difficult about basic design principles, I wanted to share with you some guidelines that may help as you design your pages.

Prioritize Your Page

As you plan your page, ask yourself: What is the most important thing that I want the viewer to see? What is the second most important? And the third? Once you have selected the top three things, accentuate them in order of importance. If you love one of your photos, make it a main focal point. If the title is significant, use the brightest colors there or put it in the most visible spot. If you've got memorabilia that you want to show off, put it front and center and leave plenty of space around it. Whatever you choose to highlight, make sure that all the other things are visually less significant.

Learn to Love White Space

"White space" is any space on your page that has nothing on it. By leaving plenty of white space on a page, your eye has somewhere to rest. Resist the urge to fill up every nook and cranny on the page.

Accent Once

If your title is already the biggest thing on the page, it doesn't need to be the brightest too. If you have a beautiful photo that is wonderful to look at, do not add a border of stickers around it. Accenting things once is usually sufficient.

Keep It Simple

This rule must be the hardest to do, but it's undoubtedly the most important! The human eye can only absorb so much information at one viewing. If you keep your layouts simple, others can enjoy and appreciate all that they see.

Choose One Style for Accents

Often it is hard to find a set of stickers, die-cuts, and patterned paper that all look good together. The photos are what the viewer wants to see. Don't add too much just to fill in the page. You should choose one set or style of accents and stick with it. If your patterned paper looks like the illustration was drawn with chalks, use chalk to fill in your title letters or shade your title block. If the stickers you are using are photographic images, then don't use a cartoon-style printed paper with them.

Artist:
Rhonda Solomon

Make the Most of Mattes

If you are having a hard time making your photo stand out, try an extra wide matte out of a solid color. I will very rarely put patterned paper right next to the photo. Often, it will compete with the photo too much. A solid wide matte sets off your photo like a piece of art.

Try Different Background Colors

One of the beauties of vellum is that it's so versatile! Changing the background color can mean creating a whole new feel. If the look of your page is not quite right, try substituting a different color behind your vellum.

Take a Photography Class

When I think of what one thing has improved the look of my scrapbooks over the last three years, I think the best thing has been taking a photography class at my local scrapbook store, Memory Lane. No matter how fabulous your pages are, if the main focal point is blurry or has poor lighting, the page isn't as pleasing. Read the manual for your camera. Take a class. Experiment. (Film is cheap compared to what we all spend on supplies.) Take lots of shots to ensure one perfect photo.

Let the Photos Decide

Not sure which colors to choose? Look in your photos. When you duplicate the colors you see in your photos, your page will have a very consistent, coherent look. If you choose colors with different values, it competes with or detracts from your photo.

Edit Photos

Can't decide which photos are the best? Ask a friend to give you feed-back on which ones you should keep. It is very easy to be emotionally attached to every photo, but limiting the photos helps you to appreciate the ones you do select.

These are general guidelines and there can be exceptions to many of them. My hope is that if you ever have a page that is not working, run through the list and see if one of these ideas will help you out. Happy scrapping!

9

Chapter 1
solid color vellum

When you're working with vellum, it's like having a watercolor palette to experiment with. Colors blend as they overlap. You can create a rainbow of colors with only a few sheets of vellum. (Look at this book's cover—only four colors were used to create the plaid effect). That's the magic of vellum: you can do so much more with less.

See the two shades of blue on "Baby Devin"? They're actually one shade of light blue layered to darken the matte around the photo – a simple technique, but very effective.

Solid color vellum feels lighter than card stock. Even with a darker blue or purple vellum you see light reflecting from the background paper. In "Flying Kites" four different shades of blue vellum are torn and also overlapped to echo the seaside colors of the photo. Colors blend well when they take on a hint of the color underneath.

clean PURE meek SOFT FRESH gentle NEW warm
my BABY. devin

Flying Kites

Vellum: Pixie Press,
Paper Adventures
Spray Adhesive
Fonts: CK Cursive,
CK Contemporary
Caps, CK Primary
Pencil: Prismacolor

Baby Devin

Vellum: Paper Pizazz
Adhesive: Xyron
(Background Stripes)
Photo Tabs (Matte)
Pens: Zig Writer
DMC Embroidery Floss
Buttons: Michael's

Flying Kites
at Carmel Beach

Lizzie Loves...

her sisters, her brother and Dad. She is always writing us love notes.

her friends. A day with friends is never long enough for Lizzie! She loves to play with Makenzie, Candice & Lexi.

to help others. Lizzie helps before she even thinks! It is a natural instinct of hers. She is very tender hearted and compassionate!

Aunt Kathie

Vellum: Paper Pizazz
Spray Adhesive
Ribbon: Offray
Swirl Punch: McGill
Punches: EK Success
Mulberry Paper: Pulsar
Fonts: D.J. Inkers Squared,
CK Gala

Lizzie Loves

Vellum: Paper Adventures
Adhesive: Xyron
Pens: Zig Writer
Heart Punch: Emagination

aunt **KATHIE**

Kathie McAffee, or "Aunt Kathie" became one of our dearest family friends. She brightened up our day whenever we saw her. The girls adored her and would rather spend a day shopping or cleaning at Kathie's house, than to spend time with a friend. She nearly always brought by a bag full of goodies when she stopped by. She has left an impression in our hearts that we can never forget.

Tips

Place punches either over or under a solid color vellum for a great "patterned paper" look.

How To

If your vellum color is looking too light, add another sheet. One sheet of yellow vellum in the top left corner was too light for the layout, so I doubled it to make two layers. This made the yellow darker so it would blend better with other elements.

11

patterned vellum

Patterned vellum papers are so easy to use, especially when you want a quick but elegent page. A few pieces of trim can be all that's needed to easily finish a page. Our "Snow Angel" page is simplicity itself: one patterned vellum background, a few punch art snowflakes, plus lavender card stock to matte the photos. Yet the result is just right to echo the beauty of fresh fallen snow.

Our examples here show how little you need to do with a nice patterned background. The pattern sets the mood for the page, but still keeps a subtle profile. In "As Good As It Gets" (p. 14), the lace patterned white background adds a playful feel, along with a formal air that suggests a wedding. Another simple page "I Thee Wed" has sensational results: the pink satin of the background hints of the elegence of a wedding day, yet it doesn't compete with the photos or the hearts.

Remember the first rule of effective scrapbooking: don't let the background overpower your photo. If you allow too much contrast or too busy a background, you risk losing interest in your photo subjects. In "Wild About You" (p.14), the bold matte behind the photo puts in a buffer between pattern and picture. Also, the high contrast of the zebra stripes is toned down by laying the pattern over a rust colored card stock.

I Thee Wed
Artist: Sharon Lewis
Vellum: Whispers by
Autumn Leaves
Adhesive: Photo Tabs
Heart Stamp: Stampin' Up
Font: CK Calligraphy

Snow Angel
Vellum: Whispers by
Autumn Leaves
Pens: Zig Paint
Pencil: Prismacolor
Snowflake Punch: Family
Treasures
Pop-up Dots: Cut It Up
Fonts: CK Handprint
CK Winter

"Teach us delight in
simple pleasures."
Rudyard Kipling

Ladybugs tickle when
They crawl up your
arm.

Butterflies have very
Long, curly tongues.

Tea parties are more
fun outside in the
garden.

When you have a
sister, you always
have someone to
play with.

Jaeda & Ajanta
Memorial Day in Pine
2001

<u>Simple Pleasures</u>

Artist: Sharon Lewis
Vellum: Autumn Leaves
Adhesive: Photo Tabs
Pens: Zig Brush
Chalk: Craf-T
Ribbon: Offray

<u>Sunny Daze</u>

Artist: Candice Cook
Vellum: Autumn Leaves
Flower Punch: Family
Treasures
Suede Paper: Nag Posh
Letter Template:
Pebbles Tracer, Classic

sunny
daze

I won't ever forget
this day. I was
trying to get the
perfect "first lake"
photo, and then,
as if you knew,
you fell asleep in
my arms. I put
the hat on, and
I had it! 2000

Maya's
WEDDING
DAY

Maya and Jesse were
married at 4:00 p.m.
on July 28, 2001.

The afternoon was
beautiful and they all
looked very elegant.

<u>Wedding Day</u>

Vellum & Stickers:
K & Company
Spray Adhesive: 3M
Fonts: CK Cursive,
CK Contemporary Caps,
and CK Primary
Pencil: Prismacolor
Ribbon: Offray

Wild About You
Vellum: Whispers by
Autumn Leaves
Adhesive: Xyron
Pens: Zig Writer, Zig Brush
Photography: Soderberg

Tips

You can tone down a strong pattern by putting a darker card stock underneath.

As Good As It Gets

Artist: Rhonda Solomon
Vellum: Autumn Leaves
Pens: Zig Writer, Zig Brush
Leaf Punches: Emaginations
Mulberry Paper: Printworks
Ribbon: Offray

Family Campout
Artist: Candice Cook
Vellum: Whispers by
Autumn Leaves
Markers: EK Success
Font: CK Voluptuous
Card Stock: Bazzill Basics

The Ricks Family

Artist: Sharon Lewis
Vellum: Autumn Leaves
Stamp: Stampin' Up
Corners: Family Treasures
Photo Corners: Boston Intl.
Other: Gold Cord, Rivets
Font: CK Calligraphy

The Ricks Family
Christmas, 1998

christmas
CUTIES
Our first Christmas picture with a boy was so fun!
The girls all wanted to hold Devin, and Devin was just happy
to be held. We are grateful for our sweet children!

Christmas Cuties

Vellum: Autumn Leaves
Handmade Paper: Pulsar
Corner Stickers: Autumn
Leaves
Leaf Punch: All Night Media
Fonts: CK Script, CK Primary,
CK Fill In
Other: Brads

creating backgrounds

When you can't find the right background for a page, don't hesitate to build your own with vellum. You've got nearly unlimited choices in mixing and matching colors, textures, and shapes. It's worth taking a little extra time to create a unique background for your page.

In Hayley's page, the color blocking technique adds to the beautiful tones of the baby picture. The border of vellum flowers is simply tied in place with embroidery floss.

"Nature Hike" uses the plaid technique found on the cover of this book. Vellum plaids have the homespun look of cloth and yet are fairly easily made. Pick out three or four colors from your photo to create the plaid.

Try matching the look and style of your accent pieces with the color and feel of the background. "Friends" has a hand-made checkered background to match the lettering style in the title. On "Happy Holly-Days," color blocking is used with decorative stitching that draws from the graphic style of the Christmas stockings in the photo.

Happy Holly-Days
Vellum: Paper Pizazz
Corrugated Cardboard:
Paper Reflections
Accents: The Berry Patch
DMC Embroidery Floss
Other: Black Cording

How To

To build up a plaid background, cut strips that are 1/2", 1", and 1 1/2" wide from different colors of vellum. Using a Xyron machine for adhesive, lay down the vertical strips first, then add the horizontal strips weaving over and under the bottom layer.

Nature Hike
Vellum: Paper Adventures
Title: Bits & Pieces by
Pixie Press
Pencil: Prismacolor
Butterfly Accents:
Ruffler's Roost
Other: Silver Studs

Tips

Sometimes it's easier to draw details on an overlaid piece of vellum. For this design, I started with a light pink paper for the background, then added 2" squares of a darker pink vellum in a checkerboard style. I then overlaid a solid pale pink vellum on top and drew the black grid lines on that layer of vellum for a smooth drawing surface.

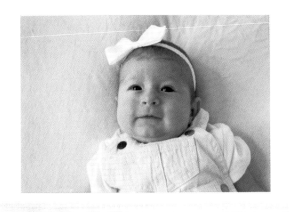

Mom and Hayley decided to surprise Dad for Father's Day. They set up their own photo shoot and took pictures of Hayley to give to Dad. Mom worked hard to get everything just right! The lighting, the film, etc. Hayley did her part too! She was all smiles for Dad!

Friends
Vellum: Pixie Press
Accents: The Berry Patch
Other: Silver Studs

Haley
Vellum: Pixie Press,
Pens: Zig Writer
Small Punches: All Night Media
Large Punch: McGill
Ribbon: Rufflers Roost
Font: CK Swirl
DMC Embroidery Floss

hayley

TEN WEEKS OLD

making mattes

V ellum is made for mattes: it's so soft and subtle, it doesn't compete with the photo. Vellum frames a picture without overshadowing, making an elegant highlight that enhances the photo.

The "Falling for You" layout has another unique benefit of vellum papers: same patterned paper can look very different depending on the color behind it. When layed over a green background (on the left side), the greens and oranges of the pattern stand out. But when placed over a yellow card stock, the pattern becomes a terrific gold and orange with light green highlights. It's two results for the price of one, and don't they look just great together!

"If Friends Were Flowers" is made up of bright colors, both in the photo and the vellum matte and background. To soften the area immediately around the photo, a rectangle of clear vellum is placed just under the photo, above the layered vellum strips. This makes a more gentle transition between the vivid background and the strong green grass in the photo. The title, too, is lifted up from the yellow by the white vellum it's printed on.

Tips

I placed a lavender rectangle under the patterned vellum matte. A plain lavender matte might have been too high in contrast. This way, the card stock is softened by the vellum and the pattern is brought out by the lavender beneath it.

Falling For You
Vellum: K&Co.
Adhesive: Photo Tabs
Pen: Zig Writer
Leaves: Black Ink
Photo Corners: Boston International
Other: Twig & Green Twine

More Sugar Than Spice
Vellum: Paper Company
Adhesive: Photo Tabs
Pen: Pentel Milky Writer
Title: Bits & Pieces by Pixie Press
Stickers: Mrs. Grossmans

My Little

daniel
age 4½

enjoyed time to walk around the pumpkin patch. He also loved picking out a pumpkin all by himself! His joy school classmate, Matt, lived there on their family farm.

john
age 2
this boy couldn't stay away from the tractor and the hay wagon! He was thrilled to sit on the hay bale and ride through the corn field to the pumpkin patch at the Day Farm.

Punkins

Tips

For an easy lettering accent, I used a border sticker with colored squares. I cut out four squares for the capital letters and inked around them. I also cut out individual squares to add instant corner accents in the journaling boxes.

My Little Punkins
Vellum: Paper Adventures
Spray Adhesive
Pen: Zig Writer
Eyelets: Stamp Studio
Sticker Border For Letters:
Me & My Big Ideas
Twine: Offray

If Friends Were Flowers
Vellum: Paper Adventures
Adhesives: Photo Tabs,
Spray Adhesive
Title: Bits & Pieces by
Pixie Press
Chalks: Craf-T

sarah and alec

if friends were flowers, i'd pick you

titles

Have you ever tried using vellum paper for titles? With vellum you can highlight titles or quotations in ways that card stock can't. Vellum also works great with stencils and die-cut lettering.

There are four ways to use vellum on titles: hand-letter the titles with ink: print directly on the vellum with a laser printer; photocopy lettering or artwork onto vellum; or place sheer vellum over a title that is printed or lettered on card stock.

In "Ready to Swim," notice how the lettering and punched dots use colors of vellum that match the colors in the photo...a simple technique can make a scrapbook design harmonious and sophisticated.

"Friends Are a Gift" uses a variety of colors, shapes, and sizes for the title word blocks. A playful feeling matches the cheery photos, and the titles coloring matches the mattes and flower stems, for balance.

In "The Best 4x4xFar," the title was inked onto two layers of vellum, with torn edges of the lower brown making a muddy base. The bottom half of the letters have a smudged look, as if dipped in muddy water!

How To
I added stems to the flower stickers
by cutting long wavy lines of green vellum.
I added a chalk line on the left for a shadow
effect, and inked dashed lines to match
the flowers.

Friends Are A Gift
Vellum: Paper Adventures
Adhesive: Xyron
Pens: Zig Writer, Zig Brush, Zig Calligraphy
Flower Stickers: Printworks

Ready To Swim
Vellum: Paper Adventures
Pen: Zig Writer
Punch: Family Treasures
Lettering Stencil: C-Thru Ruler Company

The Best 4x4xFar
Vellum: Paper Pizazz
Adhesive: Xyron
Chalk: Craf-T
Font: "Sink or Swim" by
Rebecca Sower
(Creating Keepsakes, 2001)

Tips

Note the vellum
"photo corners" on the left page.
They add an old-fashioned look
but keep a light touch
on the photo.

Just Horsin' Around
Vellum: Paper Pizazz
Pens: Zig Writer
Pop-ups: Cut It Up
Fonts: One Of Everything!
Border: Rope Design Cut
From Autumn Leaves Paper

How To

To give the title block an old Western look, I
used a different font for each letter and punched out
"bullet holes" for the O's. The first word and several
letters were highlighted with brown vellum. The title
block is lifted off the page with pop-ups.

Tips

Printer troubles? Try these two tips.
You might find that your printer won't
give good results on vellum. If so, print on
card stock and lay the vellum over it.
This works best with lighter-colored vellum.
If you want help with lettering a title,
print out your lettering on regular paper
and then put the vellum over it and
trace the letters.

chapter 6
journaling

Journaling should support the photos with color and words but not take over the design interest. Using vellum for journaling blocks is the perfect solution. They accentuate the journaling without overpowering the photo.

As you know, if you hand-write directly on the background paper and make a mistake, it's not easy to fix. Another advantage to using vellum for your journaling is that you can make sure it's right and then adhere it to the page.

Journal blocks don't always need an adhesive. Try tying a block onto the page with embroidery floss or twine, as was done on "Be an Angel" and the left side of "Sisters."

In "Miranda in Pine," journaling is printed on a white vellum that is opaque enough to block the bright designs so readability is preserved. The flowery fun of the Autumn Leaves vellum is matched by a few well-chosen punches that complement the floral and swirl designs.

Printing can be tricky. It usually works with laser printers and photocopy machines, and it may or may not work with an ink jet printer. If you have trouble printing on your vellum, you can always print on card stock or regular paper and overlay the vellum. The text will still be easy to read.

Be an Angel

Reach for the stars

Keep your halo polished

Share your favorite things with others

Say at least one nice thing to someone everyday.

Always tell the truth.

Think happy thoughts.

Sprinkle a little stardust wherever you go.

Be an Angel
Artist:
Sharon Lewis
Vellum: Paper Adventures
Paper: Autumn Leaves
DMC Embroidery Floss
Font: Gigi

How To
The photo border is made up of "squares torn from" the printed paper and then reassemb and adhered onto torn-edge mattes.

Sisters
Vellum: Paper Adventures
Pen: Zig Writer
Patterned Paper: Keeping Memories Alive
Alphabet Stamp: Hero Arts
Font: CK Posies
Twine & Buttons:
Buttons: Michael's

China Cove
beach

Many summer
vacations were spent
here as a child. It was fun
to go back with my
family. I always loved the
blue and green of the
water. It was nice to see
it hadn't changed.

...enjoying the view...

Dan, Ethan, Jacob & Isaac

Mark & Beth

...a world
to discover...

Tips

Vellum that overlaps less
important parts of photos
is a great place for journaling.
"China Cove" has torn clear
vellum strips placed over the
photo to match the waves.
The journaling was carefully
done after strips adhered.

China Cove
Vellum: Paper
Adventures
Adhesive: Xyron
Pens: Zig Writer;
Zig Brush
Stamps: D.O.T.S.
Stamp Pad: Versa Mark
Watermark

Miranda in Pine
Artist: Sharon Lewis
Vellum: Autumn Leaves,
Large Flower & Corner
Punches: Family Treasures
Small Flower Punch: Marvy
Swirl Punch: All Night Media
Round Punches: Punchline
Fonts: CK Script, CK Print

"One of the luckiest things that
can happen to you in life is,
I think, to have a happy
childhood."
Agatha Christie

Miranda in Pine
at days' end.
Memorial Day,
2001

punch art

The look of a page can be wonderfully and simply enhanced using punch art. Vellum punch pieces embellish the page and mirror details in the photos with a light touch.

The very simple accents used in "Nature Girls" makes a beautiful statement: the punch art leaves draw from the colors of foliage in the background, giving just enough balance to the left and right side of the page.

In "Little Boy Blue," Devin's blanket has yellow moons and stars in the pattern. The moon and star punch art adds a cheerful accent and the yellow vellum sets off the title with a thin matte edge.

The sun punch art does double duty on "Towel Time": it hints slightly of the warm sun drying out the kids snuggling in their towels, and it adds to the colors of the page by picking up underlying shades of blue and green. Notice how you get the two-for-one colors on the punches by simply laying them over the different background blues and greens.

Tips

Scrapbookers often punch out shapes for projects, but what about the paper they're punched out of? Punch "scraps" work great to add spice to your page.

Nature Girls
Artist: Sharon Lewis
Vellum: Autumn Leaves, Paper Adventures
Punches: Martha By Mail
Ribbon: Offray
Font: Brush Script
Photo Corners: Canson

Christmas Night
Vellum: Autumn Leaves,
Adhesive: Xyron,
Pen: Zig Writer
Tree Punch: Emagination
Eyelets: Stamp Studio
Raffia: Pulsar Paper
Photo Corners: Canson

How To

To give the page an interactive feel, I added five pop-up dots below the photo. I punched out metallic circles to cover the dots, then used very fine wire to hang the moon and stars from the dots. This gives the page interest with its three-dimensional, dangling design.

<u>Little Boy Blue</u>
Vellum: Pixie Press
Adhesive: Xyron
Pens: Zig Writer; Zig Calligraphy
Circle Punches: Family Treasures
Star punch: Marvy Uchida
Pop-Up Dots: Cut It Up
Other: Wire

<u>Towel Time</u>
Vellum: Pixie Press
Sun Punch: Family Treasures
Alphabet Stamp: Personal
Stamp Exchange
Hole Punch: Fiskars
Tags: American Tag
Photographer: Jeff Lam

die cuts

Vellum gives you a huge range of possibilities when mixing die cut pieces into your designs. Their effect is bolder than punch art and can give a sense of movement to the page.

The hearts that match the plaid shirt Andrew wears are die cuts with a vellum twist: strips of four colors are overlaid to make a plaid design (fixed with a Xyron adhesive), then hearts are die cut from the "cloth."

Look at our "First Day of School." Die cut apples, in red and white vellum, are mixed with solid red and a gingham plaid for variety. The apples are outlined with liquid pearl appliqu for a three-dimensional look —and for a hint of the fab silver glitter shoes the girls are wearing.

In "Snips and Snails", the background is made up of vellum squares arranged in a mosaic-like pattern, then dry-brushed with white paint for a roughened effect. A vellum matte softens the transition to the card stock matte under the torn-edge photo.

First Day Of School
Vellum: Pixie Press
Pens: Zig Writer
Lettering Template: EK
Success Varsity Upper
Punch: Family Treasures
Plaid Paper: Paper Adventures

Andrew
Vellum: Pixie Press
Alphabet Stamps: Personal
Stamp Exchange
Photo Corners: Canson
Heart Die Cut: Ellison
Heart Punch: Emagination

Tips

To "age" the white paper, I crumpled the paper into a ball and then flattened it out. I stamped the words onto the paper and then tore the rectangles for the matte and word blocks. I rubbed a bit of chalk lightly around the edges and across the paper —only the raised wrinkles picked up the chalk color. To keep the chalking light I worked it into the paper with a cotton ball.

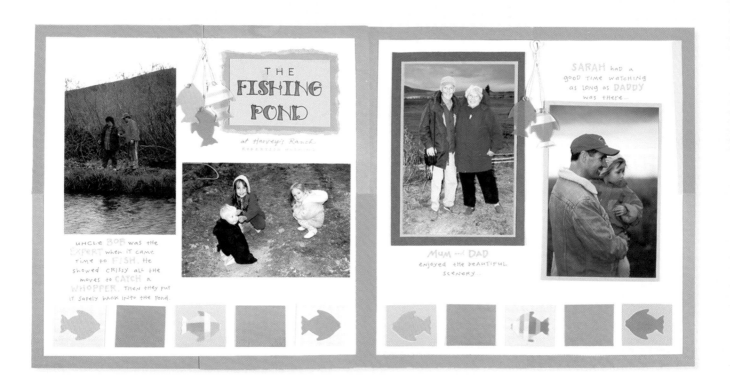

THE
FISHING
POND

at Harvey's Ranch.

UNCLE BOB was the EXPERT when it came time to FISH. He showed CRISSY all the moves to CATCH a WHOPPER. Then they put it safely back into the pond.

SARAH had a good time watching as long as DADDY was there...

MUM and DAD enjoyed the beautiful scenery...

that's what...snips and snails and puppy dog tails...

Little boys are made of...

seven months

devin

Snips And Snails
Vellum: Pixie Press
Spray Adhesive
Pen: Zig Writer
Die Cuts: Pixie Press
Title: Bits & Pieces,
Pixie Press

Fishing Pond
Vellum: Frances Meyer
Adhesive: Xyron
Pens: Zig Writer
Pencil: Prismacolor
Die Cuts: Ellison
Font: CK Gala

borders

L iven up your pages with the elegance of vellum rather than stickers or card stock on your page borders.

Notice, on these pages, how each border draws out elements from the photos. This is a basic technique that makes pages feel "right." Whether you match colors, or duplicate a design from clothing in the photo, or echo the trees in a photo background with leaf designs, you can give your page design a sense of unity that sets it apart.

In Sarah Jane's baby portrait, the flowers of the baby dress and the light lace are matched by a delicate Whispers vellum matte and a variety of punch art designs in vellum.

The charming photos on "Wildflower Princesses" need little embellishment, but the punch art flowers balance the left page with just the right touch. The vellum flower petals are made with heart-shaped punches. The flower center is made of card stock and is a heart punch cut in half.

The torn shapes of the border on "A Day at the Beach" suggest the bright designs of Sarah's swimsuit, and the bright pinks of the page background put the emphasis on Sarah rather than the neutral tones of the beach and rocks.

Sarah Jane
Vellum: Autumn Leaves
Whispers, Paper Pizazz
Ribbon: Offray
Punches: Family Treasure
Punch: EK Success

Wildflower Princesses
Vellum: Pixie Press
Adhesive: Xyron
Pen: Pentel
Heart Punch: CARL
Stems: Custom Design
Fonts: CK Tulips,

Tips

For an added three-dimensional look, double up your vellum punches. Notice how the lavendar daisy shapes are doubled: with vellum you can overlay simple punch shapes for variety and a more lifelike, interesting look.

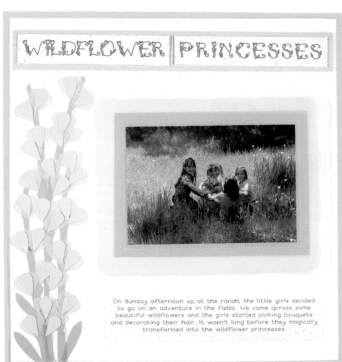

WILDFLOWER PRINCESSES

On Sunday afternoon up at the ranch, the little girls decided to go on an adventure in the fields. We came across some beautiful wildflowers and the girls started picking bouquets and decorating their hair. It wasn't long before they magically transformed into the wildflower princesses.

Rocky Point Style
Artist: Sharon Lewis
Vellum: Paper Adventures
Paper: Paper Adventures
Pencils: EK Success
Stickers: Autumn Leaves
Font: CK Expedition

The girls are showing off their
Rocky Point Style
Spring Break, March 2001

A Day At The Beach

Vellum: Paper Adventures
Pen: Zig Writer
Title: Bits & Pieces by
Pixie Press
Torn Swirls: Custom
Design

a day at the
BEACH

Sarah was so fun to watch
at the beach! She was digging
a hole, but the waves kept
coming in. She tried to
tell the waves to 'stop'
but they just kept on
coming! She had fun
anyway playing with
the soft, wet sand.
june 2001

tear art

T orn card stock designs in scrapbooking are fairly common. Rough edges have a natural feel that gives a different mood to a page. You'll see the same relaxed attitude when you tear vellum for your designs.

It must have been a lot of work to get all those white swirls on "Pocketful of Posies," right? Wrong—just one sheet of patterned vellum is laid over the page. The vellum pattern disappears over the white card stock but is highlighted by the blue. The center blue square was added on top of the vellum.

Tearing vellum can make quick work of a page: with these Fourth of July photos, all it took was torn strips of white vellum and red card stock. The blue paper with silver stars came ready-made from Pulsar, and with torn vellum mattes and red and blue card stock, the page was done in minutes.

"My Brother with Me" has torn blue & yellow vellum mattes matching the carefree style of Rebecca Sower's accent pieces. The mattes have inked-on uneven lines with squiggles to match the boats, moon, and stars.

How To

For the torn flower petals, I lightly drew a flower outline on the vellum. I held my thumbnail along the outline as I pulled the paper to make it as even as possible. I tore out two flowers and overlapped them for variety.

Pocketful Of Posies
Vellum: Colorbök
Spray Adhesive
Swirl Punch: All
Night Media
Photographer:
Richard Hirst

Fourth Of July
Vellum: Paper Adv.
Star Paper : Pulsar
Star Stamp: Marvy
Chalks: Craf-T
Other: Metal Roll
Photographer:
Richard Hirst

Being TWINS, Dalin & Braden have always slept in the same bed. They are BEST FRIENDS. They stick up for each other. If one is getting disciplined, the other will say, "Leave him alone! He's my best friend!" and then give him a hug. They play well together, and I'm so glad that they LOVE EACH OTHER.

I'd fly up to the moon

I'd sail across the sea

iF I could always Have
my brother with me

Tips

To tear straight lines, pull vellum against a ruler or hard edge. For more variation you may need to work it a little. Like all paper, vellum has a grain —when you tear with the grain you'll get a smooth, straight line, but tearing against the grain gives uneven results. It can take a little work to make all sides equally rough. When going with the grain, pull a little to one side, then the other. When going against the grain, pull slowly and don't let it get too far off the desired line.

My Brother With Me
Vellum: Pixie Press
Pen: Zig Writer
Chalk: Craf-T
Border, Frame &
Accents: Nag Posh

How To

For the title lettering, I laid brown vellum over the inked-in letters and traced the letter outlines. I then tore each letter around the outline, punched holes in the O's and B, and adhered them over the lettering.

- devin -

BOYS
and their
TOYS

- uncle nephi and the boys -

Uncle Nephi doesn't waste any time teaching his boys to love tractors (john deere, of course). He knows all about them and if you ask him his favorite color, he'll smile and say "green".

Boys & Their Toys
Vellum: Paper Pizazz
Adhesive: Xyron
Pen: Zig Writer
Rectangle Punch:
Family Treasures

stamping

Inks interact with vellum differently than the average paper. You'll find that when drawing or lettering on vellum, you need to let most inks dry for a longer period of time before you can work with the vellum. This is especially noticeable when you use rubber stamps on vellum. Stamps can put a lot of ink on the paper, and with the smooth, less-absorbent surface of vellum it can take extra time to dry.

When working with stamp ink and vellum, always test the ink on a small sample of the paper to see how well it holds the ink and how long it takes to dry. Sometimes one side of the vellum will be more absorbent than the other. Also, look for the new special inks that are now on the market specifically for use with glossy photos and smooth surfaces like vellum.

You can also try different techniques for stamping ink on vellum. If your stamp ink is too bright, try stamping the back side of the vellum to mute the color. If you want to stamp and then add color with markers, the stamp ink may smear when it touches wet marker ink. Try coloring on the back side of the vellum instead to avoid problems with the two inks.

On "Harvest Time," the flowers under the title were stamped first. After the ink had dried thoroughly they were colored with pen and pencil. A rectangle of white paper was put under the vellum to let the stamp design and photos "come forward" on the dark background.

The square and rectangle stamps by Hero Arts were the perfect background for the journaling and title of Barbara's page. The ink colors and pastel paper are so complementary to the colors in the photos.

Harvest Time
Photographer: Jeff Lam
Vellum: CTI Paper
Adhesive: PhotoTabs
Pens: Zig Brush
Stamps: DJ Inkers
Paper: Karen Foster

Our Family
Photographer: Tina Lam
Vellum: Paper Adventures
Corner Ivy Stamp:
All Night Media
Ivy Leaf Stamp: Chunky
Stamps

Tips
When you have only one stamp (such as the ivy leaf) and want to vary the results, you can stamp on the front and also on the back sides of the vellum to get a normal and a reversed image.

Our Neighbor, our F R I E N D

B A R B A R A

always filled with
PEOPLE and
LAUGHTER
because she is
loved by so many

ANGELS

Barbara has
so many qualities
that I admire!
Her COURAGE
inspires me.
Her daughter,
mother in law,

husband and
her mother all
died within
six years. Yet,
she smiles
every day
with HOPE.

She has great
COMPASSION
always watching
for those who
are in need.
(especially CATS)
Her home is

fun loving
nurturing
courageous
full of life
radiant - on the
go joyful
Unbelievable

Barbara's
friendship is
a blessing in
our lives!

Tips
When I
stamped all the squares
for this page, I let them dry
overnight before lettering
over the ink.

Barbara
Vellum: Paper Adventures
Textured Paper: Pulsar
Adhesive: Photo Tabs
Pens: Zig Brush, Zig Writer
Stamps: Hero Arts
Ink Pad: Shadow Ink

The Reeves Family
Vellum: Pixie Press
Silver Paper: Memory Lane
Antique Alphabet Stamps:
Personal Stamp Exchange
Ink Pad: Archival Brilliance
Fabric Bag: Memory Lane

stuart
julie
alexis
miranda

the
REEVES
FAMILY
december 2000

using chalk with vellum

A rtist's chalk lets you add warmth anywhere on your page. As you'll see in our examples, chalk can provide a range of subtle colors, from coal smudges to the delicate colors of a seashell.

Acid-free chalks available for scrapbooking are very different than pastels, which contain oils that will degrade the quality of paper and photos. An easy way to work with chalks is with cotton-tipped swabs or make-up sponge applicators. Also, remember not to smooth with your finger—your skin does contain oils that might mix with the pigments.

Chalk is a nice way to edge a paper, title, or matte. (See "Over the River" and the "Butterfly Kisses" title.)

In "Steamin' In to Ely" the papers are roughened up with black chalk to suggest the coal dust smudges of an old steam engine. Chalk is also used for the white clouds that echo the train's puffs of steam.

To create the mood of a soft sunrise at the beach in "You and Me," the torn vellum shells have been first drawn with pen, then shaded with chalk. (Don't add ink over chalk as it can clog the pen tip.) Chalk also adds a soft edge to the title blocks.

Bayley

Youngs Farm

Fall '00

Over the river and through the woods...

This was Bayleys first time riding a horse, as you can see... she loved it! Youngs Farm 2000.

ELY
nevada

40

On our way to California, we stopped in Ely, Nevada, at the Train Museum. Nephi and the boys were in seventh heaven when this steam engine pulled in . . .

Steamin' In To Ely
Vellum: CTI Paper
Spray Adhesive
Pens: Zig Writer,
Zig Brush, Pentel Milky
Gel Roller
Chalks: Craf-T

Over The River
Artist: Candice Cook
Vellum: Autumn Leaves
Title: Bits & Pieces
by Pixie Press
Leaves: Black Ink
Raffia: Colo Raffia

Tips

When using chalk, a light touch is usually good, bu you may find that you need to put down more chal vellum than on regular paper because it doesn't abs quite as readily. It's a good idea to test different cha and papers before making your final art.

You And Me
Photographer: Richard Hirst
Vellum: Paper Pizazz
Chalk: Craft-T
Shell Patterns: Rebecca Sower's "Bumper Crops"
Spray Adhesive

Tips

For the vellum background on this page I tore a rough edge and lined it up with the horizon line on the photos. This gives an easy visual flow to the page.

Butterfly Kisses
Vellum: K & Company
Pens: Zig Writer
Chalk: Craft-T
Mulberry Paper: Personal Stamp Exchange
Font: Lucida Handwriting

sewing with vellum

A dd some variety by sewing parts of your pages together. You can sew vellum like any other paper, by hand or with a machine.

Sewing is a useful alternative to adhesives when handling vellum. You can attach vellum titles or word blocks with a couple of stitches of embroidery thread, without worrying about whether adhesive "spotting" will show through.

For "Visit to the Easter Bunny," pink, yellow, and green card stock were machine-stitched onto the blue background paper to hold this page together. The vellum eggs were also sewn onto the pink paper.

Gold thread makes a perfectly elegant border in the "Fall 2000" portraits, matching the gold leaves. Reverse-punched leaves on the bottom border are also held in place with a few decorative stitches.

The sampler-style hand stitch in "Home Sweet Home" is a nice match for the pioneer-era house in the photos. Notice the green embroidery thread tied in a simple knot holding the journaling block to the top left photo.

Crissy
Patterned Vellum:
Autumn Leaves
Colored Vellum: Paper
Adventures
Photo Corners: Boston
International

Visit To The Easter Bunny
Photographer: Tina Lam
Vellum: Pixie Press
Plaid Vellum: Kangaroo
& Joey
Pens: Zig Writer

Tips
Crissy's page has a hand-sewn vellum envelope with an actual letter to her from Mom. As long as you're capturing memories with photos, don't forget to personalize with notes that can be read for years to come.

Fall 2000
Photograph: Richard Hirst
Vellum: Paper Pizazz
Plaid Ribbon: Offray
Pen: American Craft
Leaf Buttons: Dress It Up
Thread: DMC

fall 2000

Mom & Lizzie in front of her childhood home in Leeds, Utah.
·June 2000·

Mom told our kids that she used to hide up in the rocks when it was time for chores & no one could find her.

Home Sweet HOME

Mom's home was very humble. So is Mom. She is an amazing woman and always talks fondly of her childhood years in Leeds.

Home Sweet Home
Vellum: Paper Pizazz
Pens: Zig Writer
Textured Paper:
Memory Lane
DMC Embroidery Thread

cut-outs

I f you're unable to find the right pieces to coordinate with your vellum, try trimming bits from an extra sheet of printed vellum to use as cut-out decoration.

Cutting out shapes can simplify the work you do for a page. With just an extra sheet of vellum and background paper you can add plenty of visual interest quickly and easily.

A rose-covered background creates just about all you need for "Blossoms as a Rose." The vellum is placed over a cream card stock, which gives it an added warmth.

Rather than be limited to the printed pattern, the flowers on "Best Buds" were cut out and set free to flow around the photos. Overlapping the flowers across the photo edge helps the eye flow across the page.

In "Slicing Up," the photo matte is also laid on white paper to bring out the bright colors. When placed on the light green background, the fruit vellum was less visible.

Best Buds
Checked Vellum:
Paper Adventures
Floral Vellum: Provo
Craft
Spray Adhesive
Pens: Zig Writer

Everything Grows With Love
Vellum: Whispers by
Autumn Leaves
Vellum Title: Bits & Pieces
by Pixie Press
Embossed Paper:
Making Memories

How To

For one standout rose behind the title, I cut out a flower from the background, then darkened the edges with chalk. Once adhered to the torn cream matte I then inked the lettering over it, setting off the title block with pop-up dots.

Blossoms As A Rose
Photograph: Richard Hirst
Vellum: Whispers by
Autumn Leaves
Pens: Zig Writer
Leaf Punch: Family Treasures
Pop-Up Dots: Cut It Up

Treasure
Vellum: Whispers by
Autumn Leaves
Pop-Up Dots: Cut It Up
Pen: Pentel Milky
Gel Writer
Adhesive: Xyron

Slicing Up
Adhesive: Paper Company
Pens: Zig Brush (border),
Zig Writer (title)
Pop-Up Dots: Cut It Up
Other: Green twine

reverse and outline art

A special technique that works the best with vellum is to reverse out or outline your artwork. When you cut or punch shapes, use both the outline and the shape itself to repeat the design in different ways.

Layering colors produces synergy when you use vellum. Using tone on tone, like in "Kayla & Marissa," can add subtle accents too.

"A Real Tea Party" has flowers, leaves, and a tea cup that were cut from vellum and mixed and matched. The tea cup was cut out of purple vellum and placed over pink. On this "China Cove Beach" page, the fish and seaweed designs were cut out of the vellum with an X-acto knife. The outlines were then overlaid with a second color for variety. With photo mattes of the same three colors, the page takes on a charming, mosaic-style look.

"LAM Babies" shows another way to use outline art: the outlined letters are placed over the overlapping red and blue, matching the varsity-style Gap shirts the children are wearing.

Kayla & Marissa
Vellum: Paper Pizazz
Heart Punch:
Emagination
Swirl Punch:
All Night Media

A Real Tea Party
Photographer: Kyle Poulin
Patterns: Rebecca
Sower's "Bumper Crops"
Vellum: Paper Pizazz
Beads: Designs by Pamela

CHINA COVE beach

a day to play at

Tips

Inspiration for pages can come from many sources:
one day at Home Depot I noticed this wallpaper border strip
and fell in love with the color scheme and simple designs.
When I got back my photos from China Cove beach, I just
knew that it was a perfect fit!

China Cove Beach
Vellum: Paper Pizazz
Adhesive: Xyron
Pens: Zig Writer

LAM Babies
Photographer: Jeff Lam
Vellum: Paper
Adventures
Eyelets: Stamp Studio
Raffia: ColoRaffia

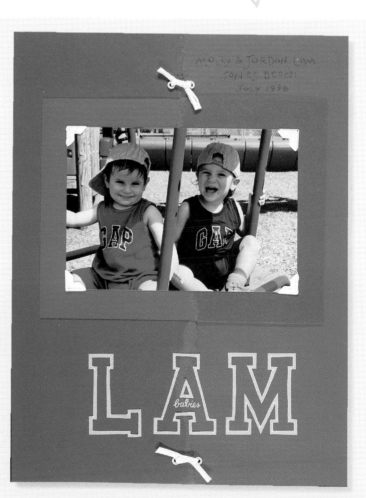

LAM
babies

vellum pockets

Vellum pockets add a fun, interactive touch that can be used for personal things, like a letter; for more practical things, like journal tags or memorabilia; and for playful things, like accent pieces. Objects in vellum pockets can tease the viewer into looking closer or pulling out the object for a better look.

On our "Mum and Dad" page, a vellum envelope holds a letter. For fun, a few confetti cutouts were dropped into the evelope. And it's held in place with clear photo tabs so it can be easily removed and opened.

Try sewing the vellum pockets, by hand or machine. The pocket on "Road to a Friend's House" was given a decorative stitch that also holds it to the page. Also, "Home Sweet Home" has a pocket that is tied to the page with light twine. The pocket holds a die-cut shape with journaling on the back.

How To

To make this pocket, measure the desired size of the pocket and then add about an inch and a half extra for the foldover flap. Emboss the flap decoration on one side of the paper, then turn it over and emboss the flower designs on the other side. Trim the flap edge to match the embossed design. For easier folding, score the vellum where you will fold it for the flap. Fold it first, then sew the pocket onto the backing paper.

Home Sweet Home
Vellum: CTI Paper
Title: Cock-a-Doodle
Design
Brads: American
Pin And Fastener
Other : Twine

A Date With Gramps
Photograph:
Tony Johnson
Vellum: Paper Adventures
Lettering Stencil:
Frances Meyer
Chalk : Craf-T

Mum And Dad
Vellum: Colorbök
Ribbon: Offray
Flower Punch:
All Night Media
Vellum Envelope: CTI
Photo Corners: 3L

Mum and Dad got married in 1953. Mum was 18, and Dad was 23. When we visited them in August, 1999 they had been married for 46 years. We are so grateful for their love for their family, and for each other.

Mum & Dad

Tips

Vellum envelopes can be useful for a lot of things: letters, memorabilia, extra photos, children's artwork, report cards, etc.

the ROAD to a FRIEND'S HOUSE is never long

The Road To A Friend's House
Vellum: Pixie Press
Fonts: CK Fill In, CK Gala,
CK Chunky Block, CK Script
Chalk: Stabilo Chalk Pencil
DMC Embroidery Floss
Other: Popsicle Stick

chapter 17
creating objects

Creating objects with vellum is like putting together a puzzle: when all the pieces are in place, it looks fantastic! Vellum is perfect for things that are naturally transparent, like dragonfly wings, stained glass, or water. The light-catching qualities of vellum make it an excellent choice for anything you would like to present in an elegant way.

As on our "Springtime in England" page, flowers can be a quick add-on if you use punches with vellum and then overlap them for subtle variety. The vellum balloons on "Happy Birthday Devin" are a natural to accent the charming photos.

There are plenty of ways to mix vellum and card stock as well. On "Summer Shopping" the little cut-out flip flops have a solid sole with vellum flowers to decorate. And the insects on the "Johnson Family" title page have vellum wings to accentuate the sheer quality of the wings

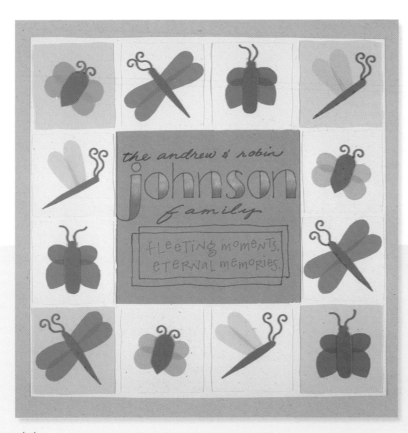

Johnson Family Title Page
Vellum: Paper Adventures
Adhesive: Xyron
Pens: Zig Writer
Pencil: Prismacolor

Springtime In England
Photograph: Tony Johnson
Vellum: Pixie Press
Punch: Marvy Uchida
Mulberry Paper :
Stamp Exchange

Tips
Think of other ideas for designs that lend themselves to vellum, such as a beam of light (from a spotlight or flashlight); a mason jar or glass vase; liquid in a glass (or virtually any use of water from waves to drops); or sheer fabrics (like a paper doll bride with a vellum veil or sheer curtains on a window).

Summer Shopping
Vellum: Paper Pizazz
Daisy Punch: Family Treasures
Chalk: Craf-T
DMC Embroidery Floss
Fonts: CK Slice, CK Script

Happy Birthday Devin
Vellum: Paper Adventures
Spray Adhesive
Pens: Zig Writer
Wire: Artistic Wire Ltd.
Fonts: Party, CK Primary

swimsuits

cover-ups

flip-flops

I learned quickly that you don't spend money in Arizona on a lot of cute summer outfits, you just buy a lot of cute swimming suits! The girls loved swimming! We swam almost every day. The cool water was delightful on those hot summer days.

How To

You have most likely seen vellum balloons before, but how about using some wire for the strings? There are great tool sets available for shaping wire. Or you can do what I did here and find 3-4 various sizes of pens. Wrap the wire back and forth around the different pens to create the free-flowing look.

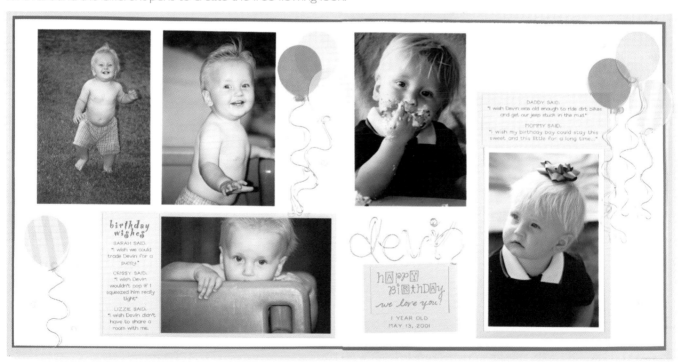

more scrapbook ideas

Now that you have seen different ideas and also learned new techniques, look beyond what's in this book and let your imagination just go. The possibilities really are endless as long as you're willing to experiment. Here are a few more ideas:

Subdue the background: lay vellum over a strong background to alive your photos breathing room. With "Solomon Family Fun" the background paper was a perfect match for the photos, but it was also a strong design that distracted from the photos. Vellum mattes take care of the problem easily.

Emboss the vellum: any time you emboss vellum you leave a white line that can add to the design. On "Devin is Blessed" the embossed lines were added using a stylus with templates as guides.

Try to vary your layers: look for ways to add interest by layering vellum in differet ways. With the mosaic of different colors on "Oh Brother," changing the placement of color blocks and vellum gives more depth to the page.

Add a photo holder: trimmed snapshots of party guests in "Birthday Fun" are held in glassine envelopes for safe-keeping. It's easy to take them out and look at them individually. (Similar envelopes made of vellum could also be used.)

Solomon Family Fun
Vellum: Paper Pizazz
Patterned Paper:
Making Memories
Raffia: Robin's Nest
Eyelets: Stamp Studio
Pens: Zig

Birthday Fun
Vellum: Paper
Adventures
Glassine Envelopes:
Memory Lane
Punches: Family
Treasures

Devin was given a name and a blessing on July 3, 2000. He was 7 weeks old. He was given the blessing by Andrew. All our family was there and we realized that Devin was doubly blessed—by the Lord, and by his great family.

baby Devin is
blessed

Devin is lucky to have so many people that love him! Grandma Pat & Grandpa Ken, Grandma Judy & Grandpa Ed, Nanna & Gramps (in England) and Aunt Lanette & Uncle Monte.

Devin is the twenty fourth grandchild.

Look at all those cute cousins!!

Devin is Blessed
Vellum: Paper
Adventures
Plaid Paper: Karen Foster
Alphabet Stencil:
Pebbles In My Pocket
Heart Stencil: Provo Craft

Oh Brother
Vellum: Paper Pizazz
Stars: Paper Reflections
Lettering Stickers:
Debbie Mum
Eyelets: Stamp Studio

How To
To emboss on vellum, you will need an embossing tool or stylus. Put the vellum on a medium-soft surface for a little flexibility. Turn the template over so you are tracing the reverse image (you're actually pressing the embossing tool onto the back of the paper). Press firmly with the stylus to leave a white line, being careful not to tear through the vellum.

OH BROTHER.

Ed

Dan

Don

Growing up, I thought that brothers were made to tease little sisters!! But I have been surprised over the years at the gentle side of my 3 brothers. Lift the photo to read my favorite memory about each brother.

invitations

S heer vellum mixed with other colorful or textured papers is a new look for invitations. Whether you print directly onto vellum and then lay it over a pattern or photo, or put a layer of patterned vellum over an invitation, you'll create the desire to look inside or underneath. Finally for a complete presentation, use plastic or glassine envelopes. Or make your own with vellum, to build interest in your invitation.

Baby Blue
Artist: Debbie Crouse
Patterned Vellum:
Whispers by Autumn Leaves
Blue vellum: Paper Adventures
Ribbon: Offray
Other: Crimped Packing Paper,
Clear Envelope, Decorative
Edge Scissors

a star is born

A Star Is Born
Artist: Debbie Crouse
Vellum: Paper Adventures
Wire: Darice
Beads: Michael's
Star Brad: Memory Lane
Pop-up Dot: Cut It Up
Font: Say It With A Smile by D.J. Inkers

Maya's Wedding
Vellum: Whispers by
 Autumn Leaves
Ribbon: Offray
Font: Lucida Handwriting
Photographer: Amanda Bowe
Printer: Tooele Transcript-
Bulletin Publishing

Wedding Photo
Vellum: Whispers by Autumn Leaves
Ribbon: Offray
Photographer: Scott Soderberg

Wedding Announcement
Vellum: Whispers by
 Autumn Leaves
Ribbon: Offray

You are invited to attend
a bridal shower for
Kristin Turner
Given by Laurie Quinn & Michele Neal
Tuesday, June 26, 2001
from 7–9 pm
come & go
at Michele Neals home
361 N Carriage Lane
814-7502

You are invited to attend
a baby shower for
the baby girl of Jennifer Phair
Thursday, May 17, 2001
from 7–9 pm
at Laurie Quinn's home
3840 S Peden Dr.
Chandler, Az.
R.S.V.P. Regrets Only
883-8481

Bridal Shower Invitation
Baby Shower Invitation
Artist: Laurie Quinn
Vellum: Paper Adventures
Card Stock: Bazzill Basics
Font: Scrap Cursive On Lettering Delights 3 CD
Ribbon: Offray
Stamp: Personal Stamp Exchange

Winter Formal
Artist: Debbie Crouse
Vellum: Whispers by Autumn Leaves
Ribbon: Offray
Snowflake Punch: Emagination
Small Snowflake Punch: Family Treasures
Wire: Artistic Wire
Thin Metal: Michael's

You are cordially invited to attend
the Mesa High winter gala
Winter Wonderland
January 15

Come and join us
to wish Jenny a
HAPPY
BIRTHDAY!

Purple Invitation
Artist: Debbie Crouse
Vellum: Paper Adventures
Mulberry Paper: Pearl
Ribbon: Morex
Other: Brad

49

chapter 20
cards & stationery

A simple phrase or poem printed on clear vellum makes a powerful cover for a photo gift. Tie it up with a ribbon to hold things in place. For a special note, try sewing something flat and small, like a dried flower or tiny word strips onto a card for a surprising, touchy-feely look. It's a small gesture that will endear your card to its recipient.

A casual way to send a note is to tear out your message on vellum and pin it to a card. Try this time-saver: on a full sheet of vellum, print or photocopy a number of phrases in a variety of fonts, leaving a half inch of space around each sentiment. Then, when you want to put together a quick card, carefully tear out a phrase and pin it to your card stock.

The handmade floral card is made with vellum and watercolor pencils. To begin, cut the stem and leaf shapes from green vellum. Then draw the flower and petals with the watercolor pencils on plain vellum. Carefully tear out the petal and center shapes, and use a wet brush to blend the flower colors. As the paper dries, the edges will naturally curl.

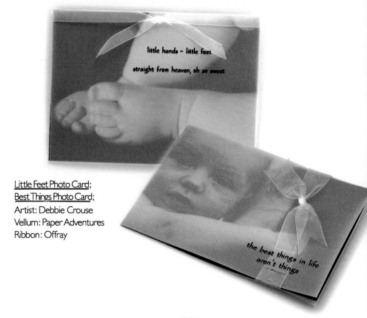

Little Feet Photo Card;
Best Things Photo Card;
Artist: Debbie Crouse
Vellum: Paper Adventures
Ribbon: Offray

Flower Card
Artist: Debbie Crouse
Vellum: Paper Adventures
Watercolor Pencils:
Sanford Colorific
Adhesive: Glue Stick

Tips
These are just some phrases that come in handy when I'm putting together a quick card. Note below where I was able to say a quick "thank you."

Vellum Heart
Artist: Debbie Crouse
Vellum: Paper Adventures
Suze Weinberg Ultra Thick
Embossing Enamel
Spray Adhesive
Other: Brads

All I See Is You
Vellum: Colorbök
Mirror: Darice
Adhesive: Glue Dots
Other: Silver Cord

Thank You From The Bottom Of My Heart
Artist: Debbie Crouse
Vellum: Paper Adventures
Ribbon: Offray

Lavender Mums
Vellum: Whispers by
Autumn Leaves
Silver Thread: Michael's
Beads: Ben Franklin Crafts
Ribbon: Offray

Personalized, matching stationery is an easy but rewarding way to share your creativity. Pieces of vellum can transform ordinary cardstock into an elegant writing paper.

The Violet Stationery
Vellum: Autumn Leaves
Card Stock: Bazzil Basics
Spray Adhesive

Floral Eyelet Stationery
Vellum: The Paper Company
Vellum Envelope: Whispers by
Autumn Leaves
Eyelets: Stamp Studio

Herb Garden Stationery
Vellum: Paper Adventures
Card Stock: Bazzill Basics
Stickers: Frances Meyer
Ribbon: Offray

51

chapter 21
bags & tags

Paper gift bags are everywhere on the market these days.
Try personalizing your gifts by making your own bags with vellum or other specialty papers. You'll find that a variety of bag die cuts and templates are available. Just cut out the shape, fold and assemble using double-sided tape to hold it together. Little extras such as matching tags or ribbon handles make your gift complete.

One special technique is to make a two-layered bag. Using the same template, cut a bag out of patterned paper and another out of vellum. Place the printed one inside the vellum bag for twice the appeal.

Violets Bag
Artist: Debbie Crouse
Patterned Vellum : Autumn Leaves
Ribbon: Morex
Adhesive: Scotch Double-Sided Tape

Perforated Bag
Artist: Debbie Crouse
Vellum: Embossing Arts Co.
Die Cut: Ellison
Adhesive : Glue Stick

Tags are a small but thoughtful addition to any gift. Look for inspiration in everyday things – or browse the aisles of a craft store – as you select materials for your tags. Simpler tags are a snap with a patterned vellum, a matching solid color background, and a ribbon or button to hold things together.

Tag Along
Artist: Debbie Crouse
Vellum: Whispers by Autumn Leaves
Pen: Zig Writer
Adhesive: Glue Stick
Wire: Artistic Wire
Chain: Memory Lane

Hope Peace and Love
Quote: Bits & Pieces, Pixie Press
Cardboard: Paper Reflections
Ribbon: Offray
Embroidery Thread
DMC

Wooden Truck Tag
Artist: Debbie Crouse
Vellum: Whispers by Autumn Leaves
Ribbon: Offray
Button: Craft Mart

Pink Hearts Bag
Artist: Debbie Crouse
Vellum: Paper Adventures
Heart Print Paper: Unknown
Ribbon: Offray
Die Cut: Ellison
Adhesive: 3L Transparent
Mounting Squares

Green Leaf Bag
Vellum: Whispers by Autumn Leaves
Leaf Punch: Family Treasures
Bag Die Cut: Accu-Cut
Adhesive: 3L Transparent Mounting Squares
Raffia: ColoRaffia

Star Bag
Vellum: Whispers by
Autumn Leaves
Star Punch: Family Treasures
Ribbon: Offray
Adhesive: Glue Stick
Other: Tissue

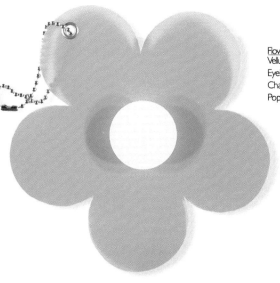

Flower Power Tag
Vellum: Frances Meyer
Eyelet: Stamp Studio
Chain: Memory Lane
Pop-Up Dot: Cut It Up

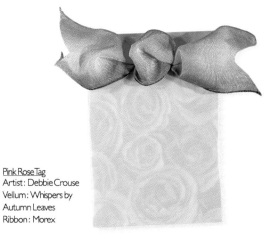

Pink Rose Tag
Artist: Debbie Crouse
Vellum: Whispers by
Autumn Leaves
Ribbon: Morex

Purple Daisy Tag
Vellum: Whispers by Autumn Leaves
Ribbon: Offray

Matchbook Tag
Artist: Debbie Crouse
Vellum: Paper Adventures
Eyelet: Stamp Studio
Chain: Memory Lane
Wire: Artistic Wire
Patterned Paper: Unknown
Other: Brad

53

chapter 22

wrapping

Gift wrapping takes an elegant turn when you use vellum. Smaller objects are a natural for vellum wraps whether they're gifts or home decorations. For example, a specialty bar of soap wrapped in a strip of vellum makes your guest bathroom look like a five-star inn.

Dress up a plain kraft paper bag with simple vellum add-ons. One bag shown here has a vellum collar and ribbon. Just punch two holes on the fold of the collar and cut a slit between them to thread the bag handles through. The blue card has a similar vellum collar with a button for an accent. You might also try using a sheet of vellum instead of tissue for a bag liner.

For simple gifts in an envelope, like cash or a gift card, you can quickly wrap vellum around the envelope to add a festive look. The Christmas ornament design was easy to trim from a patterned vellum. It was wrapped around the envelope and secured with double-sided tape. A single ornament was then cut out and tied to a bow as a tag.

Vellum works well for partially wrapped gifts, like a wrapped book with a matching handmade bookmark. Candles can also be wrapped with layers of paper and vellum and tied with a ribbon and decorative accents.

Bag With Vellum Collar
Vellum: Kangaroo & Joey
Kraft Paper Bag : Michael's
Ribbon: Offray
Button: Dress It Up

Bag With Vellum Tissue
Vellum: Kangaroo & Joey
Kraft Paper Bag: Michael's
Ribbon: Offray
Tag: American Tag

Decorated Soap
Vellum: Paper Adventures
Ribbon: Offray

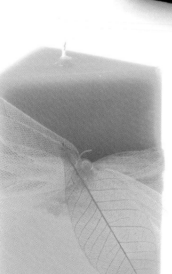

Fall Candle
Vellum : K&Co.
Tulle : Modern Romance
Leaf : Black Ink
Adhesive : Scotch Double-Sided Tape

Candle Set
Vellum: Whispers by Autumn Leaves
Corrugated Cardboard: Paper Reflections
Adhesive: Scotch Double-Sided Tape
Other : Beads, Twine

54

Silver Boxes
Artist: Debbie Crouse
Vellum: Pixie Press
Ribbon: Offray
Adhesive: Glue Stick

Just For You Envelope Wrap
Artist: Debbie Crouse
Vellum: Whispers by Autumn Leaves
Bow, Gold Thread: Michael's
Heart Punch: Emagination
Adhesive: Scotch Double-Sided Tape

Pillow Box
Artist: Debbie Crouse
Vellum: The Paper Company
Ribbon: Offray
Wire: Darice
Thin Metal: Michael's

Christmas Ornament Envelope Wrap
Vellum: Whispers by Autumn Leaves
Ribbon: Offray
Pen: Pentel Milky Gel Roller
Adhesive: Scotch Double-Sided Tape
Other: Gold Cord

Book Wrap
Vellum: The Paper Company
Ribbon: Offray
Tassel: Michael's
Adhesive: 3L Transparent Mounting Squares

craft projects

I f you like to explore new ideas with craft projects, look no further. With vellum papers and a good adhesive, you can give a refined look to an array of projects.

Decorated boxes take on a new life with the right patterned vellum. The heart-shaped gift box was first painted in a light pastel, then a strip of vellum was adhered to the base. A wreath of dried flowers on the lid gives it a vintage look.

Vellum is all about light, so a luminary is an easy idea. A glass candle holder is wrapped with a rose-printed vellum and tied with a delicate ribbon. Set in a small floral wreath, it gives a soothing, beautiful glow when the candle is lit.

Other objects, like a wooden gift box and a flower pot, are enhanced with vellum. The wooden box is simply wrapped with vellum, which is adhered with double-sided tape. The flower pot rim has a torn strip of patterned paper covered with a strip of vellum. A decorative button and ribbon are glued on to complete the look.

For a fun Christmas centerpiece, we took a tall cone from a craft shop and wrapped it in a seasonal vellum print. After curling a ribbon around it, we glued on mini clothespins to hold photos of family and friends. The vellum is held in place with sequin pins.

Cone Centerpiece
Vellum: Autumn Leaves
Ribbon: Offray
Cone: Michael's
Pin: Darice
Other: Clothespins

Heart Box
Vellum: Whispers by Autumn Leaves
Paper Mache Box, Dried Flowers: Ben Franklin Crafts
Adhesive: Xyron

Flower Pot
Vellum: Pixie Press
Paper: Anna Griffin
Ribbon: Offray
Button: Dress It Up
Pot & Plant: Michael's

Flowers
Artist: Debbie Crouse
Vellum: Pixie Press
Tag Paper: Debbie Mumm
Ribbon: Offray

Wooden Gift Box
Vellum: Autumn Leaves
Box: Michael's
Ribbon: Offray
Adhesive: 3L Transparent Mounting Squares

Luminary
Vellum: Whispers by Autumn Leaves
Ribbon: Offray
Wreath: Ben Franklin Crafts
Adhesive: 3L Transparent Mounting Squares

bookmaking

Personal books, journals, housekeeping books, and handmade photo albums are just some of the ways you can put vellum to good use. Use it to decorate a plain book, or bind your own book with sheets of specialty papers.

An easy start is the camp journal shown here. A plain stitched book with rough-textured paper becomes personalized with a special cover and title page. The card stock and vellum on the cover are held with copper brads.

A simple booklet made of folded paper has an elegant cover made with a sheet of patterned vellum. One leaf in the design is highlighted by placing a torn square of white paper between the vellum and background paper. The booklet is bound with twine looped through three holes.

A more ambitious project is the home journal. This includes a variety of vellum and other papers held together with a plastic binding. The heavy cover wraps around like an envelope flap to keep the contents together. Inside, some pages are folded over for pockets to hold paint samples or fabric swatches – handy to carry with you as you look for decorating ideas or plan a new color scheme.

Scrapbooks are great for photos and memories, but what about those bits and pieces you collect along the way? Try making a vellum envelope book that is tied together at one end with ribbon. (Because of this binding, you'll need to cut a slit in the envelope flaps so they will open.) Fill the envelopes with vacation reminders – ticket stubs, matchbooks, small maps – anything you want to preserve in a tidy place. Or make a shower memories book: hand out cards to guests at a baby or wedding shower and let them write a piece of advice for the mother or bride to be. Then collect the cards and save them in an envelope book.

You might also try a handmade album. The album pictured is made of lightly textured cream paper with a vellum cover. The pages are stitched together at one end, and the binding is decorated with ribbon and small beads. The ribbon was looped through small holes punched in the outer binding strip. The beads were strung on white thread, which was also looped through the holes.

Camp Journal
Vellum: Whispers by
Autumn Leaves
Punches: Family Treasures
Book: Target
Thin Metal: Michael's
Other: Brads

Leaf Booklet
Vellum: Whispers by Autumn Leaves
Paper: Bazzill Basics
Other: Twine

Rose Album
Vellum: Whispers by
Autumn Leaves
Paper: Memory Lane
Ribbon: Offray
Beads: Michael's

Home Journal
Vellum: Frances Meyer
Button: Dress It Up

Envelope Book
Vellum: Autumn Leaves
Ribbon: Morex
Envelopes: CTI Paper
Eyelet: Dritz

frames & mattes

Take the framing ideas you learned in the scrapbooking sections of this book and apply them to real-life picture displays. A little vellum can do wonders for a plain frame!

Two inexpensive wooden frames are enhanced by a rectangle of patterned vellum. Cut the vellum to fit within the frame and apply spray adhesive to hold it in place.

A plain paper mache frame becomes much more with some speedy additions: the frame was first covered with a sheet of vellum, then a ribbon and a framing row of beads complete the picture.

For a sweet baby picture, cloud-patterned vellum is placed inside a wood frame, with a square cut out of plain vellum to frame the photo. Edge buttons were glued for added charm.

Inside a clever Plexiglas frame, a square of patterned vellum makes a background, and a photo is trimmed in a small circle to fit in the flower center. The photo and background fit between the two layers of Plexiglas.

Floral Frames
Vellum: Whispers by Autumn Leaves
Spray Adhesive
Frames: Ben Franklin Crafts

Before

After

Square Kraft Frame
Vellum: The Paper Company
Frame: Michael's
Ribbon: Offray
Beads: Designs by Pamela

Bloom
Vellum: Hot Off The Press
Spray Adhesive
Quote: Bits & Peices by
Pixie Press
Flowers: hand-pressed
Frame: Target

Flower Glass Frame
Vellum: Frances Meyer
Plexiglas Frame: Habitat

Cloud Matte
Vellum: Whispers by Autumn Leaves
Buttons: Dress It Up

Conclusion

I recently met a friend who had taken a vellum class I taught about a year ago. She had decided after the class to do an album with vellum on every page. She brought her album to show me what she had created, and when I looked through her book, I was amazed! She had done all sorts of things with vellum – things I had never thought of or taught about. I was so impressed with her talent that I asked her to share a layout with us for the book. Michelle Yaksick's sample is what you see below.

The other sample is from a designer at C-Thru Ruler Co., Sharon Kropp. At a recent convention, she showed me their new templates (Déja Views) for making realistic banners and ribbons. I loved her sample using vellum and asked if I could share that with you. The look is beautiful!

You have seen in this book how vellum can be used for every aspect of your scrapbook page. Vellum can do anything cardstock can (except be opaque!). You can use vellum for so much beyond scrapbooking that I hope you'll try something fun and creative. I just wish I could see all that you create!

Thanks for letting me share all this with you and have a wonderful time discovering the joy of vellum!

Artist: Michelle Yaksick

Artist: Sharon Kropp

About the Artist

Robin Johnson grew up in Kaysville, Utah. She attended Brigham Young University and the University of Utah, graduating from the U with a degree in graphic design. Robin was introduced to scrapbooking eight years ago by her sister Kris. Since that time, she has taught classes at stores and conventions across the country and was selected to be a Hall of Fame winner by Creating Keepsakes in 2000. She has also designed 3 different product lines that are all produced with vellum.

Robin and her husband Andrew have four children Clairissa, Elizabeth, Sarah, and Devin. Robin named her design business "Starlit Studio" because she does all of her work at night when the kids are tucked safely in bed and the stars are out.

About the Author

Dan Maryon has been a technical writer, editor, and also a publications manager for 15 years. After his sisters persuaded him to try scrapbooking, he started a travel journal using photos from a trip to Europe with his wife, Dorothy, in 1999. After writing this book with Robin, he's going to take that scrapbook apart and start over. Dan and Dorothy have three children (Kate, Rachel, and Ethan) and live in Orem, Utah.

For more information
about Autumn Leaves
and Whispers, including
a retailer near you,
call 1-800-588-6707
or 1-818-986-7384.

good night...